Care Bears™

Sweet Dreams

Funshine Bear

Share Bear

Grumpy Bear

Wish Bear

Tenderheart Bear

Bedtime Bear

Love-a-lot Bear

Friend Bear

Cheer Bear

Good Luck Bear

Published by Modern Publishing, a division of Unisystems, Inc. No part of this book may be reproduced or copied in any form without written per_____blisher.
All Rights Reserved.

Modern Publishing
A Division of Unisystems, In_
New York, New York 1002_
Printed in the U.S.A.

Series UPC# 49590

D1211124

Heart Cookies

Mid-Morning Nap

Cloud Car

1. FIND THE REAL BEAR

Look at the four pictures of Tenderheart Bear. Only one is the real Tenderheart Bear. (Hint: He is the one that is different from the others.) Circle him.

See Answers

Tending the Garden

Afternoon Fun

Get Well Soon!

2. COUNTING

Look at the groups above. Circle the group that shows five. Put an X over the group that shows three. Draw your own group of four hearts.

See Answers

Sending Sweet Dreams

Watch out below!

Ready or Not...

3. A BIRTHDAY PRESENT

Cheer Bear is wrapping a present for Tenderheart Bear's birthday. Connect the dots from 1 to 30 to see what it is.

See Answers

Painting a Portrait

Picnic Fun

4. COUNT THE FLOWERS

How many flowers do you see on the trail? Write the number on the line.

See Answers

The Perfect One!

Starry Night

Making Wishes

5. HIDDEN HEARTS

Love-a-lot Bear has spilled some hearts from her bucket. Help her find them by circling 10 hearts in the picture.

See Answers

Smile!

Good Company

Today's Mail

START

FINISH

6. SHARING

Share Bear has a special heart-shaped balloon to give to Bedtime Bear. Help Share Bear get to Bedtime Bear by following the correct path through the maze.

See Answers

Raindrops

A Concert

7. ALL ABOUT YOU!

All of the Care Bears have tummy symbols that tell something about them. In the space above, draw a symbol that tells something about you!

Engine Trouble

"Anybody need a hand?"

8. DOT MOBILE
Connect the dots from 1 to 27 to see what this
Care Bear is traveling in.

See Answers

"And one for you…"

It's fun to hug!

9. YOUR FRIEND

The Care Bears are good friends. In the space above, draw one of your good friends. Why do you like this friend? What do you share?

Hats

A seed will grow.

10. WHO IS SLEEPING?

Fill in every space with a dot to see which Care Bear is sleeping.

See Answers

Care Bears on Parade

Funshine Bear reads a book!

11. FIND THE MUFFINS

Friend Bear made apple crumb muffins but the muffins are hiding. Find and circle 10 muffins hidden in the picture.

See Answers

CARE - A - LOT

_____ _____ _____

_____ _____ _____

_____ _____ _____

_____ _____ _____

12. MAKING WORDS

How many three-letter and four-letter words can you make with the letters in Care-a-lot? Write the words on the lines.

See Answers

Hiking

"We love you!"

Rolling In the Clouds

A New Year

A Cloud Bear

13. MATCH IT!

Look at the things on the left. Draw a line from a group on the left to a group on the right with the same number of items.

See Answers

Delicious!

Painting

Snow Day

14. HELP GOOD LUCK BEAR

Good Luck Bear's four-leaf clover disappeared from his tummy. Draw another one on his tummy.

See Answers

Group Hug

Invitations

Reading Buddies

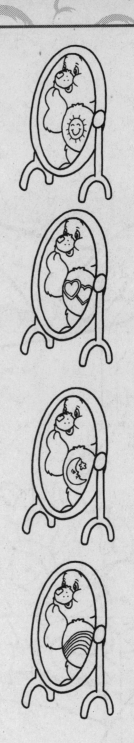

15. MIRROR IMAGES

Cheer Bear, Funshine Bear, Love-a-lot Bear and Bedtime Bear are staring in a mirror, but their images are not in the correct order. Draw a line from each bear on the left to his or her image on the right.

See Answers

Around and Around

Party Fun!

Follow the Leader

16. PATTERNS

Look at the pattern in each row. Choose a picture at the end of each row that continues that pattern.

See Answers

Grooming

A Big Heart

17. WHAT'S WRONG?

Some items in the picture are out of place. Circle the five objects that don't belong in Care-a-lot.

See Answers

Rise and Shine

Start

Finish

18. FIND THE PAINTBRUSH!

Tenderheart Bear dropped his paintbrush while painting rainbows. Help him get to the paintbrush by following the correct path through the maze.

See Answers

Team Work

Jump for Fun!

Something smells good!

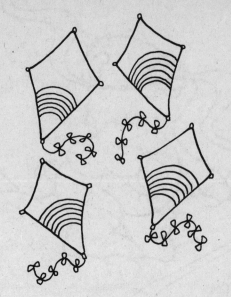

_____

_____

_____

_____

19. HOW MANY?

Look at the groups above. How many of each group do you see? Write the number on the line beneath each group.

See Answers

20. LOVE-A-LOT'S PROJECT

Love-a-lot Bear is making Valentines for the other bears. Circle the four items that she will not need.

See Answers

Evening Songs

Everybody wins!

Friends
Sunshine
Flowers
Picnics
Breakfast
Four-leaf clovers

21. LISTS

Good Luck Bear is making a list of good things. On the blank sheet of paper, make your own list of good things.

Holding Hands

22. PRESENTS

It's Bedtime Bear's birthday! Look at the presents. Circle the one you think is the best present to give to Bedtime Bear.

See Answers

A Busy Day

23. DIFFERENCES

Look at the two pictures of Bedtime Bear. Circle three differences between the one on the top and the one on the bottom.

See Answers

Surprise!

Two by Two

24. MISSING LETTERS

Look at the sign. The vowels are missing. Find and circle the missing letters in the picture and write them in the correct spaces to tell where you are now.

See Answers

Start

Finish

25. PATIENCE

Grumpy Bear is waiting for Cheer Bear. Follow the correct path through the maze to help Cheer Bear get to Grumpy Bear so she can cheer him up.

See Answers

Till Next Time

ANSWERS

1.

2.

3.

4.

5.

6.

ANSWERS

1.

4.

2.

5.

3.

6.

ANSWERS

8.

12. CARE - A - LOT

Some possible answers are:

car	eat	late
cat	let	real
are	race	cart
tar	rare	tear

10.

13.

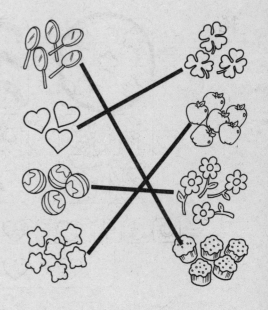

11.

14.

ANSWERS

15.

17.

16.

18.

19.

2   4

6   8

ANSWERS

20.

23.

22.

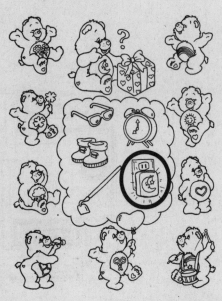

24.

25.

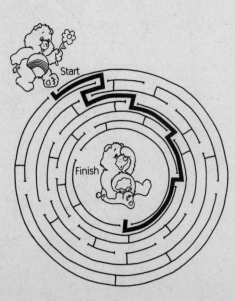